When Silence knocks, Will you answer?

By: Eudese-Elisabeth Willins

Published By Books of Hope Boston
A Collaborative program of Lena Park Community
Development Center.

Program Director: Tyler Barbosa
Editors: Lauren Miller
Cover Design: Tyler Barbosa
Interior Design: Tyler Barbosa
Printer LuLu Publishing

Books of Hope Boston 150 American Legion Hwy,
Dorchester, MA 02124

Copyright © 2017 by Eudese-Elisabeth Willins
ISBN
13: 978-0-9994382-1-3

Printed in the United States of America

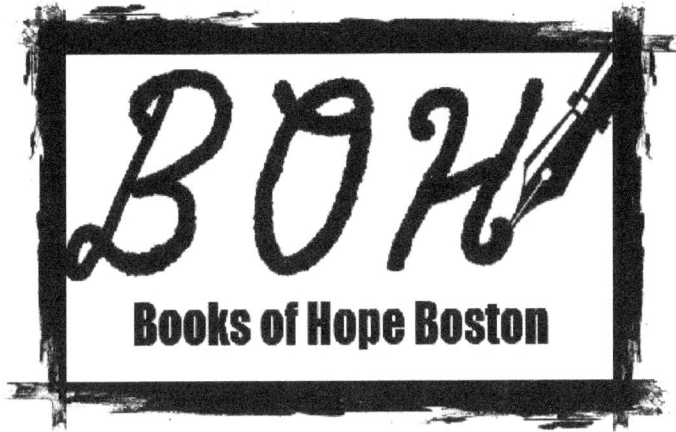

Books of Hope Boston

Our Mission

Books of hope Boston (BOHB) is a literacy empowerment program that brings creative writing workshops to at-risk urban and immigrant youth and adults in the communities where they live. Our mission is to inspire and create a safe space for the next generation of authors, artists, poets and writers .

<u>*Dedication*</u>

To the two Queens who fed me the strength
that I have within me today.
To Boston where I was raised.
To Rhode Island where the real Journey began
wakening the early morning talks.
To late night speeches and life lessons that spoke poetry to my mind
body and soul.

Table of Contents

Intro

Chapter 1:Knock Knock

Chapter 2:Who's There?

Chapter 3:Loveosity

Chapter:4
All Lives Matter But Here is Why Black Lives stand out

Chapter 5:Will you Answer?

Chapter 6:
Today this is me
Tomorrow I will have more
growth

GOD
Hmm
Battle And Balance
Carnival
Ladies night
Shoes & Lipstick
Power
Today I Slay

INTRO

Warning

They say the same thing that makes you laugh can make you cry
I will need you to laugh to stop from crying
Sharper than a knife my word's may be the cause to your wound

I apologize for all the words I never spoke
For their ink to drip from your ears
Gently kiss your lips

I apologize that you will discover me
See me, visual who I am for the first time
We can't turn the hands of time
But my poetry will give you
The first time feeling
The first time you held me
The first time my laugh met your ears
My smile left a print on your soul
My story will have you see me
See who I am for the first time
Like the day I was born

I was told never to air dirty laundry
Well I am wet and I hang myself in my writing to dry out
Talk and talk type and type write and write until the words in me
Leave a piece of the real me with you

Haven't written in awhile A poetic free write

Haven't written in a while
Like a child waiting for their father
Words haven't come to visit my paper

I haven't written in a while
Like a lost teddy bear, no sleep happens without
I cry out at night thinking of all the stories these tears could tell

I haven't written in awhile
My pen's ink has been running cold
Shivering scribbling scrambles of on and on nothingness out into the blank

I haven't written in awhile

Chapter 1- Knock Knock

Could You Be Me

Could you be me?
Could you wake up like I wake up?
Try to stretch and stand but your leg goes numb
Could you be me?
Convince yourself to turn the other cheek
Though the other cheek is just as sore
Just as bruised
Just as stained from tears
Could you be me?
Quenching your thirst with your own blood
Squirting from your tongue
Pierced professionally by your own teeth
Stories emotions untold
Could you be me?
Bringing your heart to a gunfight
Shots fired
Buckling at the knees
Begging the air that you breath
The voice that you speak
Not to fail you now
Could you be me?
Recognizing that it could be worst
But it don't numb the pain
I'm human and I do hurt
Could you be me?
If I were a challenge
Would you accept it?
Could you be me
Whooping your own ass
For every time
You walk into the fire
Questioning your own
Intelligence
Duh how did I not see that coming
Could you be me?

Constantly telling yourself
You knew better
Yet questioning yourself
Why didn't you do better
Could you be me?
Just for one day
Just for one hour

Can You Hear Her

Voices in my head
Screaming shouting crying
Control
Smiling laughter
A story untold
No sound
No voice
I can't hear me, can you?
Hear my words
The ones unspoken
Hear the people that live within me
Can you hear when she is happy?
Sounds don't only play when she is angry
Do you hear my smile sneak across my lips
It's louder than any anger that makes a bed out of my face
Is my laughter heard?
Like the tweets of the bird outside your window this morning
I am not always angry
I am not always hurting
But when I am, do you hear that too?
Without me using my voice to tell you
Do you hear me?
Notice me?
Is your love the sound to my system?
Can you represent, defend, when I can't stand for myself?
Can you hear me?
I'm speaking
Now, respond.

How Am I To Know

I know of love between mother and daughter
I know of love between grandmother and granddaughter
I know of love a family can only give
How am I to know of love that rings bells
Releases doves, sings songs, where the heart skips a beat like an
overplayed Record?

How am I to understand what is suppose to happen between woman
and Man?
How am I to carry my purse full time,switch from my running shoes
to Classy heels
Let my ponytail loose?
How am I to cook breakfast with nothing but his T-shirt on?
No rush or care in the world to beat the work clock
How am I to just sit on the throne, wait for the food
When what I know is to go out and hunt?

How am I to understand how to love a man?
When what I was taught is, I'm your mother and your father
To love a man is more of a reason to love myself
Early mornings breakfast was cooked and served by a woman
Shortly after, that same woman rushed out the door
Couldn't be a minute late, because that's a minute out of a check
A minute short from paying for those picture day memories

It was best sung if you wanna know if he loves you so it's in his kiss
How am I to know the worth of a kiss?
The meaning of a hug
The importance of a stare, or glance?

How am I to appreciate what I never been shown?
How am I supposed to be a mirror and reflect it giving a man
All that a woman is suppose to give?
I don't understand how to make you feel wanted or needed
I don't know how to boost or stroke the ego

I don't understand how to tend to a man mentally or emotionally
In what way am I supposed to know?
How am I to control my need to control?
How am I to take a break and hand this operation to my business
partner?
How am I to love and respect a man
To wear a skirt instead of the pants ?
When a woman took out the garbage late nights
A woman worked a 9 to 5 and then an 11 to 7
A woman signed all the checks paid all the bills
Brought home the food and cooked it too
All while raising me

Did I tell you

On the inside of every notebook words of encouragement filled a blank canvas
Xoxox mommy loves you

Did I tell you I come from a good home?

Sometimes lunchables, other times sandwiches, kool aid jammers, a fruit, and a snack made with love in a paper brown bag.

Did I tell you I come from a good home?

Summer camp,summer jean jackets and chucks in every color, back when jean's came in corduroy.

Did I tell you I come from a good home?

Jesus, jesus jesus I got him on my mind. Toy microphone in my hand and a broom in hers singing and praising early Saturday morning.Laughing together, watching I love Lucy. Watching me flip through pages of the dictionary because what does this word mean She could of told me but life isn't easy and answers aren't handed to you.So search.

Did I tell you I come from a good home?

Good bye kisses and hugs as little me rushed out with my tweety bird back pack filled with lisa frank notebooks, pens, crayola crayons, color pencils, rulers, and all back to school. We believe you are an A+ little girl.

Did I tell you I come from a good home?

Family dinners I didn't eat until food was blessed. I didn't eat until mommy and Nana were seated at the dinner table with me. I didn't eat until we were the Picture perfect family at a dinner table eating fresh off the stove food, while I Rambled on and on about my best friend and what we learned at school.

Did I tell you I come from a good home?

My life is written on pages
How did it end this way?
I was loved
I was protected
My family is innocent
Did I tell you I come from a good home?
Did you know it was my choice to leave at 17?
Did you know?
Did I tell you as my life is written on pages read by eyes I may cross only once?
Just know I come from a good home, Even a good girl has to stray away and Grow up

Chapter 2 - Who's there

Her Name is Eudese

Night creeps in with daylight in it's shadows. Feet move back and forth as hands on a clock. Whispers breeze by her ears,thinking she is too old to believe that monsters are creeping under the bunk bed that she shares with a strange face in black. No sleep tonight. No sleep forever.No sleep until she no longer shares a bunk with the face unknown, until bedtime lullabies are not moans of women pleasuring themselves in order to smile,that even in the shelter by the crazy house there is some pleasure in the hand they were dealt. Tossing and turning. Tick tock, tick tock. Is the sun still sleeping? All of this time to think. All of this time to turn back. Once the sun rises and the van parks with doors open to freedom, all this time to run back home. A nose bleed breathes some light in the darkness. Where is life going? What is home?Home felt like tip toeing around bombs with the intent to explode. If she didn't belong home, If she was not one of the many pieces to the puzzle of the shelter, where did she belong? Only 17. only a scooby - doo duffle bag only $40 hidden in a special pocket. Only her arms protecting what she knew to be her life. Only her in this bunk bed in this shelter by the crazy house. This was not her ending, this was the start of her page one. How do I know? Because her name is Eudese.

I Am Not For Sale

I am not for sale
I am not for free
I roam these sidewalks
I roam these cold streets
I focus my eyes
my tired, swollen, sadness runneth over eyes on
White and yellow lines painted on the road

Men, strange men, honk their horns
Roll down their windows
Men, these strange men, yell things
They make offers
They ask how much I am costing
They comment on my walking
 My curves, like the roads they are driving on
They comment
They stop
They stare

My pocket's are empty
Lint packed it's suitcase
Took the paintings on the walls
Leaving my pockets bare
Money is floating from rolled down car windows
My stomach grumbles, the wind picks up
Pushing me
Shoving me
Smacking me
Roaring in my ears
Smacking me the burn the sting set's in
Like a batter women I am ready to fall,
Holding my apple red cheeks, praying the wind didn't leave a bruise
Rubbing my cheeks , praying the wind didn't leave a bruise

 Money still flapping out the window

Temporarily feeling the heat coming from the car
Slowly thinking about the food I can buy with what he is waving
Maybe I can rent a room?
 Afford a roof over my head
Purchase a new curling iron for school since my old one was stolen
from me
This is the portrait of desperation
A soft pillow to rest your head on
Warm food to cuddle your stomach
Hug your nose with it's aroma from the spices flying free in the air
As the fire burns from the stove
Keys swinging from your belt loop as child swinging from monkey
bars

This is what desperation sounds like
Screams that echo through the night
Dried coughs, from a dried throat as dried as crops that haven't lived
through a month of rain

Desperation is me
Homeless with no destination
No steps to walk upon
No doors to lock and unlock
No keys hanging out my key chain attach to my belt loop
This is desperation
No Showers to spend hours in
Steaming up the mirrors
Just a sink and a minutes before someone rushes in to use a stall
Just a wash cloth kept in your bag, trapped with no place to hang and
breathe
I am desperation
I may be desperate,but I am not for sale
I am not for free

Never Good Enough

Toothless smiles
Twinkle Twinkle Bright Eyes
Keep swimming Keep Swimming
Keep running Keep Running
A Crescent moon , proud fire candles lit await you

" Daddy Look a B - "
" I got a B - on my math test ".

Smile still toothless
Bright eyes still twinkle
I swam to where he stood
I ran to where he waited

" A B - where is the A + you know better"

What I knew was I did my best
What I knew was I gave it all that I got
What I knew is that proudness within myself tasted like
Melting Ice cream in a cone
Felt like burying my feet into the sands of a beach
Dipping my little piggy toes into cool waters
What I knew was from a D to A B -
I wasn't good enough for you be proud of me

I share this to say this
Protect your treasures from the poisons that have spilled in the sea
For even gold can fall off its pedestal and tarnish

Ramblings of Just a girl

Word's drunk driving on a wet road
I am just rambling on
I am just singing a song
I am telling the story, people no longer read
Unless it's written on facebook, no matter what we can not abandon
speech

Do not mind me I am just rambling on
The middle maybe the end
The end maybe the start
That start maybe the middle, just remember I am just rambling on

Closed drawers held secrets of journal entries And pack bags
Carpets carried my tears
Walls could talk, four white walls with pictures of shero's were
witnesses
I left because slamming doors and loud voices
Tip toeing on that thin line that separates love and hate mother and
daughter I refused to be the cliffhanger in between my lines

I'm just rambling on
Straight A's and B's with the exception of a mathematical D
Crossed out innocent until proven guilty
I was just guilty of plagiarizing words out of an anatomy book
Labeling it a project
I was the young adult behind bars
I'm not taking a plea
I'm not saying it was me
I am Innocent
Minus that failed MCAS grade in math
In schools good behavior doesn't get you out
Walking across the stage like walking across the pavement of
freedom
Fair to say this is the first time the system SCREWED this young
Black Queen

No child left behind act isn't a privilege given to the struggling but still trying Black
Don't mind me I am just rambling on

Till this day I couldn't tell you if it was love or illusion
I can't tell you if it were real or fantasy
Bare with me I am a writer we are society's crazies
I can tell you all the stories, tell you all the times,
Remember the taste of my tears, sounds of a cracked heart but that part of the story stops here remember I am just rambling on
This poem is a box of chocolate you get what you get
Listeners can't be choosy it's my ramblings

I will tell you sex has so many meanings
Just not what is written in the dictionary
What your parents tell you about the birds and bee's it's just beautiful wrapping on a gift they don't want you to see
Lust is a cage with a lock
Hormones can be thieves in a candy store, people that find your wrapper sweet some just look but there is that one that wants to slip you in their pocket without permission
Keep your camera on for a full pocket when leaving your business establishment
It may just hurt you what they try to take when they know you are your own security
Yet I'd be rambling with a blanket of lies if I didn't ramble sex has beautiful portraits as well
There's many sides to sex's stories
But I'll stop here
This is the end of my rant
I'm just a girl rambling on

Chapter 3 -
Loveosity

Forgive And Forget (Part 1)

A broken record on replay, I find myself trying to drag forgiveness
out of me
Visuals of you and her
The sound of the music blasting
Drinks pouring
Your body as clay, mixed together close to hers

You are my man, but that night she made you hers
It's the part of the movie that I can not stop pressing rewind

I keep telling myself to forgive you
I pack a suitcase
Bras
Panties
Socks
Shirts
Jeans
How many do I need?
I should just pack everything
I'm not coming back

You kissed her
You shared what is mine
It's like she is now a part of me
I look at your face
Bright red lip prints on your lips, cheeks
They don't lay on your skin perfectly
These lip prints don't belong to me
I keep telling myself to find forgiveness in my heart
Forgiving isn't enough
I need directions on how to forget
Your lips pressed against mine dose not feel the same
I know it was just one time One kiss
One mistake
Too many drinks

Too many puffs of weed
My eyes weren't deceiving me
A witness near by me confirmed what I wanted to ignore
How do I forget while I continue to love you and hate you with one foot out the door?
How do I forget that my kisses were shared?

I was told people only remember the bad that you do
However I remember the good man in you
I remember the times you surprised me at work
I remember the nights you rocked me to sleep
Held my hair back as my emotions threw themselves in the toilet
I remember the good in you
I remember why I love you
I remember you bending on one knee
I screamed out yes I do
Can I really let one girl take you away from me?
When I know she meant nothing, despite you giving her exactly what you give me The one person I know means everything

His side of the story (Part 2)

The alcohol held a gun to my head
Weed was threatening to pull the trigger
Blame it on the liquid that eased its way down my dried throat
Not quenching my thirst, but leaving a trail of blazing fire
I'm burning with lust and desire

Blame it on the smoke clouding my judgement as it filled my lungs
Blame it on the alcohol the rocks the henny
Blame it on the loudness of the weed that pushed my lips upon hers
Just don't blame it on me

Soberly let me tell you that I am sorry
Let me kiss you
Hug you
Let me tell you that I love you
Just accept it

Meanwhile you're sipping
Pouring drink after drink
Stumbling
The evil you digest can't erase how much you love me
Posting my picture
Misspelling your words
So drunk your typing has a slur
Everyone gets the point even drunk you love me
That is you though
This is me
I kissed her
I lifted her body up
I held her in my arms
I spun her around
I took a test drive on her lips
I kissed her with the lips that you kiss

I blame it on the music

It was grinding time and she was so close and lust I forgot you
I forgot that you, my woman, was our audience
I forgot that the round of applause was coming from you
I forgot that I told you that I am in love with you
I am sober now
I remember your smile
I remember your scent
I remember your voice
How you feel in my arms
I remember that I love you
I'm sorry

In This Room

By the wall, you cornered me
By the wall, you stopped understanding me
My anger became your energy
You dug your fork into me and fed

On the bed, you sat
On the bed, you questioned
On the bed,we exchanged spirits
You snapped mine in half
You no longer wanted me
So you returned me back broken
Why did I stay?
Why did I allow myself to love you?

My tears have landed on this floor
A trail of diamonds you have crushed with your bare feet,
Not an ounce of my pain was exchanged for you to feel how tight my
boots are on my feet

By these stairs, you grabbed me
By these stairs,in this doorway, your hand raised beyond the moon
and the sun
Eyes filled with stars
You knocked the clouds out of my sky

It was this sidewalk you threw your words at me like stone
My heart crumbled painting your stones
You were to blind to see love dripping out on the very sidewalk you
stormed

It was this train station that reminded me why I brought love a ticket
away from Me
Love wasn't suppose to live here
Then you came along
Now here I am writing this same poem

I am hurt
I trusted you
I believed in you
Believed in me
Believed in us I loved you
Why would you do this to me?
Sounds familiar? Yes? Because nothing is new under the sun

His Love Is

My learning lessons
My amen blessings
Lips
Cheeks
Hands
Sharing is caring
And though I'm not Irish
Kiss me
He does
Developing my language
I'm in love
He does
His strong intense stare
Something like a smooth summer breeze
Yet a mysterious uncertainty of what the next season will bring
We are now
I am here
Notebook with scribbles of his name and mine
He is my teacher
Our one on one session has begun
I will always stay after
I will always stay forever
Every minute and moment shared is an experience well learned
He deserves my undivided attention
With the unconditional knowledge is given
Holding my hand within his we create our own world
Our kingdom
He showed me paradise
I now know what love tastes like
Tutor me where I am weak
Build me up where I am not strong
Repair me where I am broken
Let me watch and observe
I am his student
Quite ignorant, oblivious, to what love is

I am learning
His love
I am gaining knowledge of a love I never understood

Never was quite able to grasp
Now I sit in his class
Tick tock tick tock
Time is endless
Time stops and stares
Distracted by him
By his lessons
His examples
Experiments
Are never ending
Just as he taught me
Love can be and will be many things
As the seasons come and the seasons change
They never end and neither will our love

When Do You Feel My Love

Is it during the kiss shared in a rainstorm?
The splashes of water against our skin as we dance in the puddles on
the ground   where our feet meet

Is it during the cold nights?
The nights when the wind roars, rushing you home
Is it during that one moment of mental warmth as you pull your coat
closer to you?

Do you feel my love during the first sip of hot chocolate?
Whip cream on your lips like a kiss

Is my love felt during the long walks on the beach with the summer
breeze strolling right by your side?

Do you feel my love when your toes meet the golden sands?
When the sun kisses the ocean when it is ready to set?

Is it felt when a butterfly kisses a leaf?
A ladybug hugs a shoulder?
A bumble bee whispers sweetly to a blooming flower?

Is it felt when a puppy embraces its owner?
In the first glance from a mother to her child?
In the proudness a father finds in his son?
When a family goes unbroken?

Is my love felt during the loud arguments?
Silent make ups
Strong stare's that see right through you?

Is my love felt through life?
Through laughs?
Through all things beautiful?
Is my love felt then?

<u>Some Nights</u>

Some Night's I want to dress up
Just for you
Just for me
I want to dress up
Meet you at the front door
Leave a " Follow me this way " trail of clothes

Some Nights I don't want to talk
I just want to let me hair down
Just for you
Just for me
I don't want to hear the knocks on the door
I don't want to hear the angry car horns and over worked cell
phones
I want to hear your whispers in my ear
I want to feel your chills go down my spine
I want to feel your skin against mine

Some nights all I want is you
I'm selfish
Fiending for you
Can you find my clues?
Open my hidden door
I'm an unsolved mystery
Anxiously waiting for your conclusion

Some nights I look forward to your
Fingertips mixing in with my melanin
Singing jazzy blues to my soul
Massaging your secrets into my skin
I only turn my pages for you to read

Some nights bring me to a place ,Where I feel like I just can't
get enough of you
Some nights I just need it to be you and I

Chapter 4 - All Lives Matter but here is why Black lives stand out

IceCream Truck

The ropes still swings
Hitting the pavement before the light up sneakers and sandals hit the
ground

Basket Balls still bounce up and down the sidewalks
Mother's yelling after their son's from the porch sending warnings
about not Chasing the ball if   it rolls into the street

Grandmother's continue to plant in their garden's humming their
Favorite tune
While keeping a trained eye on their grandchildren, who are cooling
off in the Summer heat
Tossing around water balloons

The young women still strut in their short shorts
The young men walk around wearing polo's shorts and fresh new
Kicks

Summer still lives on
But the Ice cream truck don't ride around here anymore

Strawberry shortcake's
Snow cone
Cotton candy swirls
Cry babies
Mega missiles
The ICE CREAM TRUCK don't ride around here anymore

Loud sirens out sing the boom box on old man Jenkins's porch
Red and blue light's cover the brightness of the sun
Everyone begins to run caught in a cross fire, a few bodies drop

Ropes are no longer swinging, balls are no longer bouncing
The last water balloon was popped by a bullet , now it's raining
Blood is spilling all over the sidewalk's and the street's

If only if only the ice cream truck ….
But the ice cream truck don't ride around here any more

A mother cries out to the heavens as she rushes to her son
She thought she hoped she figured he was running for that ice cream truck
But the ice cream truck don't ride around here anymore

Louder siren's more ambulance drive into the neighborhood
Grandmother's wishing and hoping for a new sight
But the ice cream truck don't ride around here anymore

Survivor's for another day run to their homes
Eye's glue to their window's
Peeking behind the curtain blind
Watching the siren's flash
The ambulance drive by
But no ice cream truck
Because the ice cream truck don't ride around here anymore

Born in War

August 21st, 1991
Born with duct tape on my mouth
Hands tied behind my back
I was born with a condition
See I born with Black Woman
And yes, it's genetic for my mother is a black woman too
But either way it appears that I lose
Because there is a war on women
And a war on being black too
Neither is acceptable
Words written to be a woman is a curse to be black is a sin
Well, call me a sinner
I will never apologize for the skin I am in

 I have an understanding
 There is something ugly about the lips these words seep through
There is something hideous about the nose I breathe through
There is nothing society approved about my knotted locs

The sway in my hips places a horrible taste in other's mouths of
The curves and shape that I have developed should make me want to
crawl under A rock and hide never coming out until my body
somehow gets it white ,I'm sorry I meant white I apologize again I
meant right
That I should never be seen until I am ready to fall to my knees
Surrender saying I am sorry but you will never get that from me

I was Born In war
Born with intent
But see I have this understanding that
While I am to hate me
I am to praise the beauty
Of tanning and needle injections
Of butt lifts and implants of breast
I am suppose to support and applaud the talent

Of a person with a doctor who can create bigger lips
Idolize the Kylie Jenner of the world
And the Kim K's who are making cornrows famous
I remember those being slave braids, wouldn't that fall under being black
Tan's wash off, my skin you can throw all the water at me
In 2- 3 business days my skin, my beautiful skin doesn't fade

Yet either way I roll this dice
There is still an issue because I am woman
I've been made cripple during this robbery
My voice being taken away
My mind being put to sleep
Force feeding me to accept that
I am down to nothing
That men are women
Women by name
Women by the change of their birth certificate
Women by a pill feeding hormones that are meant for me
Hello I was born with a vagina naturally
I was made to have ovaries
Made to be able to carry a baby
I was made to bleed monthly for seven days a week
I was born this way naturally
And here is everything I know being robbed from me
And placed in the hands of a man
Laying on a cold surgery table screaming I am ready to be her
And what kills me
Is that it's awarded
To the Bruce jenner's I mean Kaitlyn Jenner's,been a woman for 24 hours
And somehow you win an award for being a woman for a year

My skin is my weapon
My grandmother prepared me for a war like this

I offend you without saying a word
I scared you without jumping out at you
You hate me all while I welcome you to my art gallery
Where I am all over painting's
 Artist admire what I didn't need an injection for
Artist that are probably your son's and daughters
Spend hours mixing the oil paint's to be precise about
The beauty that there is In a Black woman

All the years of pointing fingers
That same hand pulls cash or credit from your wallet, paying for
these pictures
To place in your living rooms
Plastic surgeons on speed dial
Letting me inspire you
Place food on your surgeon's table
Because you just have to have these lips
My lips

shhhhh remember I have duct tape on my mouth you heard nothing

Dear Black Folks

Caution Caution
Yellow tape surrounding
Camera's out and we begin recording
Black lives matter
Black lives are burning
Turning into black ashes
Being blown away with the wind
Abandon buildings is what black lives have become
Burnt by a torch being held in our own hands ,lit by our own lighter

Red hand prints left on the walls
Caught red handed is what it is called
The white man's plans
Is it really though ??
Or do we not want to find a solution
So we say it is all the white man's fault
Try to force ourselves to believe it's so

Scrolling scrolling
Click click
Fist are being thrown
Legs are kicking
Scream's of curse words
Hair is pulling
Braid's are flying
The expansive weave that cost
Three pay checks is falling to the ground
Guess it's not sewed in as tight
As the grip that is placed upon the black girls
Neck by another black girl's hand
Fighting over the young black boy
Who can't seem to find value in respecting
Potential black queen's
Which is crazy because he came from a black queen
So you'd think you'd really think .....

I suppose the clothes being ripped
The boobs and dingy panties exposed
Is all the white man's doing
At least because I am black I am suppose to believe it's so
However there is something deep within me shouting no no no

A few quotes to slowly come to an end
If you do not respect yourself why should I?
If you do not love yourself why should I?

Dear Black folks
Pouring the gasoline
Igniting the fire
Up in flames black lives are burning
No call to 911
Google inbox is searching world star hip hop instead
Clicking on the facebook apps to post up a new videos
Witness to the scene until the red and blue flash
Run behind our curtains
Reciting to our young ones snitches get stitches
Too late because your face is on camera someone done shouted your
name
Video is spreading fast like a wildfire
Yet it's the white man's fault
For not showing up
To solve our problem we created

Queen's In Training

The day I cut my hair word's of my grandmother I cut my strength
Know that your hair is your crown
Your kinks and coils are the lines your story is written on
What a beautiful story it is, Even when the word's turn ugly there is beauty
Remember It is not what they call you, It is what you answer to
You are a Queen a Goddess do not answer to anything less than

Your Melanin is Kissed by the sun
Darken by the night skies that the star's shine in
Queen In training you shine
Queen in training you rise
Queen in training there is not another like you
Walk with her head held high for there will be plenty that want to clone you
Have you abandon the art work God gave you
So they can scream they are the originator of your beauty
Just for that reason embrace and love what you have naturally
You are Not europen, your beauty does not need to rise to their standard's
Your beauty rise higher
Your Beauty, your Elegance reaches beyond the sky for your mind knows
Beyond the sky there is the moon stars and solar system
Queen in training my vision is your view
Never a princess in honor of you
Never a main character sharing your truth
Never a line telling you to love you
I was once a little girl like you, Wondering why Barbie's hair is straightened
Yet mines roars and growls fights back with combs and brushes
Tangles coils and kinks, I know realize my hair is my strength
So Now as a young woman who was once like you I can tell you

Queen In training you are you, Learn yourself
Never allow someone to define you
Tell you who you are
Just walk in a room your natural beauty will glisten
Heads will turn Mind's will open, People will listen
For you are a Queen in training and all Hail the Queen

Chapter 5 -Will you answer ?

You Remember This Day

Cross your T's Dot your I's
No matter who lays their eyes on your beauty
Walk with your head held high

This world is your book
Read where words lay
Search for missing words between the lines
Highlight the things you do not understand
Years later you will look back
And speak the words I now know what my Nana meant

Remember this day
Remember the dates
Of all our talks of 25 years
Many more to come for even when my body lays to rest my spirit will
walk with you

Remember this day
Remember where we sat
Remember what no one and I mean no one can take from you, your
education

Remember this day
Remember this afternoon
Remember this night
I share my knowledge
For I am always looking out for you
Remember , I will never allow you
To slither down the drain
Remember that I love you
And even when you don't speak the words
I know you love your nana too

Train Ride Back

As if frozen, my fingers tremble
My hands shake
Nervousness fills me as water fills a cup
Fear enters me as I begin to enter this stage of life
Where I travel back in time to allow this storm to brew
From the cold glass window I lean my head on I can see from afar
The grey skies, the clouds bunching together like the story
Replaying in my mind over and over constantly thinking
Contemplating are some stories better left
Untold unwritten????
Your honey filled voice wanders in my mind
Your hum's of Gospel
Your smiles
As we sit in the golden yellow pineapple kitchen
For your morning lectures
My morning lessons, as you will always end it off telling me
And you remember that it was on this day that I have shared my
wisdom with You
Hand's still tremble as the next stop 14 16 22 street approach
The bell screech's DING! My finger is on it
The train stops
I wish he would have stopped
I wished my voice was louder than a church bell
I hoped that my hits my pushes my shoves where stronger
Than a mother gripping her child's hands crossing the street
I wish fighting back it wasn't enough, I wished that I could have ran
home to you
And let you be the napkin's to my tears
Let you be the band – aid to my wounds
Let only the love that you could give me detox these poisonous
moments   out of The pit of my stomach
Where they continue to rot
But I couldn't no matter how many time I shoved my fingers down
my throat Hoping to vomit the hushed secrets the story that I never
spoke to your ears

I wished all the nights I laid on a bench before sleep hushed me looking up into The skies that a shooting star would fly freely with the birds reflecting itself in my Dark eyes I wished that the days I fought for my virginity I protected my voice For even at this moment as the train stops , as I watch my steps my feet hitting the pavement as my body did so many times after digesting what you told me was the good the bad and the ugly

I wanted my stomach acids to push this secret out of me

Causing me to hurl over and spill it letting huge chunks

That never sat with me to well splatter on the walls so my echoes could tell you What I couldn't

But here I am on this train ride back

Here I am stumbling slurring like a drunk

Mumbling like a child afraid to ask a question

I guess I haven't grown up yet

You never did but please don't judge me

I know you never will but please don't love me any less

And hopefully you will understand I never told these stories

Because I always wanted to see you make the sun shine with your smiles

I always used your glow to shelter me from the hurricane that my umbrella was Too weak to go against

I'm sorry you had to find out this way

For you and I never held no secrets

Ballerina

I was once a ballerina, Your ballerina
Pretty in pink
My tutu fluffed
My ballet shoes newly pink
Freshly laced, picture perfect pointed toes
I was once a ballerina, your ballerina
Mommy's little ballerina
I twirled in your love
I curtsey to your smile
I was your ballerina
You were my number 1 fan
You rooted for me , you cheered for me
You shot up from your seat like a shooting star
Your claps roared louder than thunder for me
Always I heard you through the applause
Through the cheers
That's my ballerina
That's mommy's little ballerina
But What happened ?

I was once a gymnast, your gymnast
You watched me flip from mat to mat
I fell but your love pulled me back up
I continued to flip and fall until it was done right
I practiced my balance
Every night I limped
I cried from my massive swollen ankles
The next day I was back at it again
Masking my pain because I was your gymnast mommy's little
gymnast
My leotard so cute
My pillsbury dough girl belly poking through
Your camera was always flashing
Your proudness was like a warm hug at the end of each performance I
felt it I Embraced it

I was your gymnast, mommy's little gymnast
But what happened?

I am now a poet
I am now a writer
Every open mic a seat is left empty
I speak, I perform, I tell stories
My words fall upon every ear but yours
My words touch many hearts but yours
Through the applause
Through the cheers
I hear silence
Flashes of the camera so bright so I am blinded
Hugs are given
The embrace isn't the same
The proudness that nourished me with courage is like a child's game
of hide and Seek I can't find it
I am now a poet
I am now a writer
What happened

Maybe

(Reference song : You are my sunshine - Beach boy's)

"You are my sunshine my only sunshine
You make me happy when skies are grey
You'll never know dear how much I love you
Please don't take my sunshine away"

Maybe she cradle me at night
Sweet kisses on my cheeks
Sweeter than my dreams
Maybe she shared her stories
Her ink writing her words on my heart
Convince me to keep my head up
Look both ways before crossing
Maybe she spent 20 mins guessing what my scribbles where
Maybe she read a pocket for corduroy
Every morning noon and night
Maybe she lost her voice
Shouting until I understood right from wrong
Maybe she tells me I love you
Making me believe that love is all you need
Because she is my mother

Maybe she shared make belief stories of gold , so I can know see
when words of others turn green

Maybe her words fell silent upon my ears
So I can become immune to life's pain
I can fight for my last breath
Before losing it
Even during a blackout
I gained strength and not death

Maybe she said the phrase I won't
Just so I will
Maybe she repeated the phrase I can't

So I can, and as I say it's done

Maybe possibly she said no
So I can figure it out on my own
Maybe she pushes me away
For as she always says one day I won't be here
And when that day comes shed no tears
I'd understand to stand on my own
Maybe she left me with memories
That comfort me
Because she is my mother
And maybe just maybe that is her way of loving me
Her way of teaching me
Her way of guiding me
Sometimes love hurts, that doesn't mean it's not real
I love you mom
Some don't have a mother to argue you
But while I have you , I want to love you in every way possible
After all you only argue when you care

Discovery

I rode my bike until I fell scraping my knees and elbows
I sat down on the curb with a bottle of bubbles to blow , but never was
I waiting On you

I stared outside of the window when the snow fell to cover the
pavement
When the sun shined light on the ladybugs and the fluttering
butterflies the Daisies daffodils and sunflowers in nana's garden , I
had expectations for the ice Cream truck to drive down my street but I
wasn't expecting you to come onto our Porch ring our doorbell and
ask for me

I didn't miss you because I was taught not too
I didn't love you because I was shown that I wasn't suppose to
I didn't ask of you because I was told that we didn't need you

As I argued on the debate team about how a father is not needed
How a fatherless home has no effect on the child as long as a strong
woman is There to do what she is suppose to do as a mother and to do
what the father Couldn't do as a dad the child will turn out ok

I used myself as an example always ending my debates with I turned
out OK
My eyes would search the audience my mother smiling proudly
Plenty of parents disagreeing with me, but what did it matter? I
walked away With a trophy

 High fives and recaps of my technique to my grandmother
There was no room to realize that as I sat on the surgery table at 12
years old that You wasn't around to say goodbye to me before I was
consumed by laughing gas And put to sleep

Over all the high notes hit while screaming happy birthday to me, I
didn't realize Your absence while I blowed out my candles and made

a wish , I wasn't wishing For you I actually wanted my wishes to come true

A bus ride home a little girl sat with her father
Smiling from ear to ear her toothless grin was beautiful
Her hair bows matched her dressed and colorful striped stockings
Her shiny black shoes swayed back and forth
She rested her head on her dad

Flashbacks of being a child
Bus rides with my mom resting my head on her arm
 Eyes slowly closing
 Nudges to keep me awake our stop was next

My eyes closed just traveling back into time
"I love you daddy" her high pitched voice screeched
Snapping back into reality
My eyes stayed focused on this little girl
Stayed focused on her father
Her father began to smile ear to ear
Identical smiles except he had his pearly whites
He pushed her loose hairs away from her face
He gently kissed her forehead and responded "I love you too"

Neither of them knew it but I smiled with them
I made myself apart of that moment, Not realizing a bitter taste was entering My mouth that my eyes were starting to water that I was beginning to form a Lump in my throat not realizing something was happening to me, something that The best way to control it was to swallow that lump and turn my headphones up A Little louder

Friends posting birthday baby showers and wedding celebrations with their dads

My friends sharing stories of their childhood
It was my father that taught me how to ride a bike
It was my dad that showed me how to roller skate

I don't know how to roller skate
I don't know how to ride a bike

I remember watching "Steve Harvey" take his daughter out on a date
Expressing how it is important that she knows how to be treated by a
man
So he takes her out he opens doors he pulls out chairs he lets her order
first he Reminds her how beautiful she is   they talk for hours about
whatever she wants To talk about That lump in my throat
That bitter taste in my mouth
The water in my eyes return again
But then I remember I'm not suppose to cry for you
So I swallow it all down and turn the channel to something else

One day I couldn't swallow the lump
I couldn't get rid of the bitter taste
I expressed I screamed I shouted I rolled my eyes I sucked my teeth
I hated you like I hate needles
I hated you like I hate math
I hated you like I hate putting laundry away
I was hurt by you
I was hurt at the fact that you robbed me
I was hurt that my mother was an accomplice
I was hurt that there wasn't even a story as to why for me to hang out
to
I was hurt that I hated someone that I didn't even know
And what I didn't know was a part of me
I didn't know you , so there was a part of me that I didn't know

Now here we are today
I brought you a birthday present
I lived for your smile and approval
Just as that little girl did when she screamed to her father that she
loved him
I wanted your hugs and I got one
I wanted the same kiss on the forehead
I wanted a moment and that is what I got

On carnival day when I showed up to your job
Dressed in my costume you gave me a huge hug
Told me that I looked beautiful
Admire my costume admire me
Told everyone that I was your daughter
And your proudness of me I felt

And though I am no longer a little girl I am now a grown woman
And there is no way we can travel back into time and place you in all
the Moments that you missed out on
I guess you weren't needed then as you are now
Every day we are blooming like a flower in a garden
Thank you for not crushing our growing flower
One day I maybe able to scream out I love you dad
Maybe one day I will have that moment just as that little girl on the
bus

Aunty Ann

A chance to say farewell, since I've already spoke the words Hello Aunty Ann, I'm Graduating Aunty Ann, I would love for you to be there Aunty Ann

This is a dedication poem, I will forever save an empty seat for you at my shows Poem, I will tell everyone about you poem, even though the last time I spoke to You was July 2015 and only GOD knows when was the last time I stopped by to See you poem

This is the poem where the words are the tears that haven't sung a goodbye song To my eyes yet, A poem where I thought Christmas was not the same anymore, Santa forget about you when you ask to have school loans paid off poem, or plane Tickets to London poem

This is the Christmas will not be the same because I came to visit you December 25th 2016 When I found out that you passed away last year December 2015 poem

This is a poem that will come to life and speak the stories I can't speak I Remember the scent of grilled cheese sandwiches rising from the oven and zebra Cakes was my favorite poem

 Dragon tales and read between the lions was always the music of life coming From the living room mixed with laughter, conversation and toys being played With from us kids poem

 I remember how you would either wash my clothes, or put me in another set of Clothes so I can go play and get dirty because aunty Ann my mother expected me To be clean when she picked me up from daycare poem

I remember how you would redo my hair whenever the Barret's decorated the Lawn poem just so my mother wouldn't notice not a single loose strand poem

This is a I can still see all of us daycare children taking turns riding the scooter Down the hill, starting from the back of the house to the front poem , I remember The pair of Jean sandals you brought me one summer poem, A first time I ever Smelled collard greens poem this Is my I will always remember you poem this is Dedicated to my aunty Ann poem, all though I am going to say rest in paradise , I Still can't believe GOD has called you to be with him poem, farewell Aunty Ann

Future Husband

Dear Future Husband
Could I let this poem express
How my love over flows the cup?
How my love spills on the floor
Like milk?
Should I just recite my love for you?
Will your ears listen
When I say I'm not traditional?
The song goes first comes love
Then comes marriage
Then comes the baby with the baby carriage
But I'm not traditional
So allow me to paint the ways
To remove my glasses sitting comfy on my nose
Share my vision with you

Dear Future Husband
Love will come first
See the issue is the marriage and then the baby carriage
I want the baby carriage and then the marriage
I want my future child to not just be told my story
But to be a part of my I do's
I want my future daughter to see how love should seek her
I want her to decorate the sand with seashells
And when your tear meets the beach
I want her eyes to capture the tears journey

Dear future husband
If we have a son, he will need a Curriculum on how to be a man
When you plan on bending that one knee
Make sure like a math problem you explain to him how you solved
your equation
I want him to be a straight A in love with happiness
So pull out your chalk board

70

Educate him on his suit and tie
Educate him on how a knight keeps his armour shined
Show him how hand's work opening doors or pulling out chairs
Show him how ears nestle stories of those long days
Drop knowledge on how he can count the ways of love
Make sure he walks the road of manhood
Carrying a briefcase of your lessons
Make sure he isn't the reason someones daughter stains her skin like
glass
Make sure his hands don't create the sound of a shattered heart
That echos through a broken woman
Make sure he understands to love her as his mother is loved
Dear future husband
Love will come first
Family will follow
And then I will express my I do's on loving you
The old man smiled
His eye's closed
My word's carried him to a time he once knew
Not to be nosy young lady
But share this love share this knowledge
So here I am writing this letter to you
Dear future husband

When you were Just a dream
Eudese Elisabeth& James Bonner

Dedicated to our future son or daughter for one day you shall be born and this is for you.

I wonder will your cries create melody sweet like kisses, Warming me like poetry to tell me you love me in the middle of the night

I wonder will your eyes racing the sun, Coo's and laughs giving birds it's sweet tweet and melody be the word's of encouragement that I will need to share with you some day

Will you be my little sunshine or my bright moonlight? Will we read that one special book countless times to you and the stars that shine in honor of you being our creations

I wonder will your crayon's develop into pen? Will your construction and scrap paper's become story pages? Will your scribbles become words, will you speak and speak because all the words in the world have not experienced you yet, Or will you observe be the quiet one that makes friends with curiosity that puts the discover in mystery, That makes the but why's and how comes the song we sing even when you aren't there

You haven't even made it into my arms yet and I already feel my arms around you. I can feel myself hold you in the sky as the sun's warm rays kiss your cheek. I can already imagine her you and I on the beach laying idle on a blanket on the sand. The soothing rush of waves washing every care in the world away. The cool breeze putting a giggle filled smile upon your face; these are the moment's I dream of

Believe it or not you have exceeded my expectation's. You have made me proud. You have captured my heart. I can only imagine the impact you'll have when

To the child who broke my heart

Anger was his step
Hate was his stride
Defeat was his voice
I heard his cries
I saw the tears that he didn't let escape his soul
His tears cut through my melanin
I oozed out our history on the pavement that we once built

He is only nine
I hear his cries
He has no knowledge of his history
He has no understanding of the depth of his story
He is ignorant to the fact he is a king in training

His words "I hate being black"
Blowing in the wind
Nestling into ears of blonde hair and blue eyes

"I hate being black
You have the nice blue eyes
You have the light brown hair
You make the girls sing about those blue eyes
But I'm just black"

"I'm just black
And there is nothing special about being black"

My tears met the grey skies
My tears bounced off of weak clouds
My tears rained down
My heart skipped a beat
Words of my mind filled in the quietness
What if that young king was my brother?
My mind drew a blank

Emotions filled up empty space

Like how scribbles from a crayon fills paper
What if he was my future son?

What if he was a kid I knew from my neighborhood?
What if he becomes that kid that dangles from a tree limb?
Tear stained dear family letter
What if he becomes the new black face on the news?

I just pushed the stroller
Of white babies with blue eyes and blonde hair
For that's what I get paid to do
Just what if?
This poem is to the black child that broke my heart
This poem is to the child that doesn't know that a piece of him runs
through me
Day by day I try to repair that broken piece within me hoping
someway
Some how
It heals him

Thank you

Reference - The script - "Breakeven"

Every word she spoke her voice drips gold on them
Kind is a name for a fool

I didn't know that the thin line between love and hate is actually invisible
When the teenage me who believed in every teen R&B pop song that
I grew up listening to, thinking this love thing has to more than words grinding on rhythm
Erupting bomb like emotions in the home of my treasure chest

I was told, but I didn't know
I was told, but you where the real teacher
You turned facts into knowledge and like a sponge I soaked it up
So thank you

Round of applause
My hands are free from carrying your niece
Born to a father tatted up with whips and handcuff prints on his wrist
And a mother so high she didn't need the needle in her spine
She had several in her arm

Too high to realize rubber is what makes bands
And bands are what goes on the end of her little girls hair after braids and beads
Thank you
My hands are free to exchange a shake with yours
I waited for the bus
Babysitting not with myself in mind but with us
Carrying your blood with me so I can put clothes on her back and clean diapers On her bum
Since her mama was just mentally trippin' on life
Thank you
Kind is the name of a fool

Thank you
If you lay with a dog, you gonna get back up with fleas golden
I was told but i didn't know
I was told but you were the real teacher
When I was trying to build our foundation
On education
You were just rolling when poisonous lips said roll asking how high
when the Devil in silk jet black curls demanded you to jump
You were playing in dirt laying on poison oak
You was busy getting tangled in webs
While I was searching the webs for my degree
Yet you didn't care about me
All I got was an apology
And a burn when I pee
Oh and despite being a teen aiming for a degree in childhood ed and
psychology
Ms.Willins you can produce a degree but never a baby
If you lay with a dog you will get back up with fleas
Thank GOD for a pill
I'm released from your demons

If english is not understood let me thank you in spanish gracias,
You welcomed me with your lessons so in return for my thanks
silence is louder Than any your welcome your lips can speak
Thank you
 In between a crack heart is a lesson learned and a teacher who
taught, as the line in one of my favorite songs when a heart breaks it
don't break even

Words to myself

Dear Eudese,

Sincerely from Eudese. Surrounded by childhood pictures and memories. I ask myself what advice would I give the younger me? I stand here at the age of 20? What words would I share with me at 14? What would I have warned me of at ten again I'm thinking dear Eudese sincerely yours Eudese I think and finally I cry.

I envision little me sitting in front of me, waves like the ocean slowly turning into a curly puff of cotton candy wrapped in a beautifully colored bubble, soft deep brown eyes inviting everyone into my imagination, getting a front row view of my curiousity. Displaying my mind as a child proudly so open to life. Not a scar or a sad story to tell living within.

My Smile is huge enough to run competition with a half moon on a beautiful summer night. I envision me as a child as a ten year old girl still stuck in her world of barbies books and tonka trucks. The same girl who grew up admiring "Pocahontas" and "Mulan" for their fearless attitudes I envision little Eudese, Then my eyes open I see little Eudese replacement who little eudese has become

I see me a much older Eudese. Locks the color of gingersnap cookies, knotted up tightly like a rope. My scars I wear oh so visibly, permanently like a tattoo I thought was cool at 16 and by 20 seen all the mistakes in getting it.

My sad story laying in my heart but living in my eyes waiting to be told loudly either through a story or a live performance of poetry.

I see me the one who once admire fearlessness now living life fearful ..... Fearful of love because love can turn into hate fearful of hate because hate is the cause of loss of loving me, fearful of success because the higher you climb the harder you can fall and there's always someone trying to knock you down .

Had I known at 10, 10 years later this would be little eudese would I want to even grow up too be me ?

Words to me.

Words too the younger me coming from the older me, no need to think again I said if at ten had I known this would be me would I want to grow up too be me?

You see at 14 I remember screaming and shouting for help. My voice ranged through the empty school halls like the school's fire alarm Can you hear me? I remember fighting my robber Trying to hold down the crook trying to protect everything I had in my safe . He almost got away with everything worth something . The V-card is very rare, see the little Eudese was only 14.

Would I still want to grow up to be me? If I understood that I would become victim to a drug Powerful than anything you can sniff or swallow. All I had to do was look and I would feel the feeling that up till this day is unexplainable, But knew it was my weakness because I craved yearned for the same thing everyone wants to once experience Love.

I needed it morning noon and night I needed to see it visibly there I needed it to fill me up mentally physically spiritually and emotionally it was that strong that addictive that at 18 I said here's my heart you can take it here is me I want you to have it but had I known of the addiction and poison that was being hidden, little me Little me I'm a victim now because of a gift I couldn't keep wrapped up.

The looks of love is truly blind, deadly when it deceives you. His looks were so good his words so strong he told me I would love him and I listen. Followed my heart to be deceived. Though deadly what he had only bruised he didn't kill me. Today I'm still alive because today I have the vision in my mind And little Eudese in my view looking up at me as I look down at the little girl I once knew. I see the hope that I lost during a field trip where I would loose me if I could tell little Eudese how much I failed her, becoming homeless, Surviving hungry nights, Daydreaming during hungry moments, Sleeping during class because I kept my eyes open all night for my job and the travel to another place that made me feel like I was doing time for a crime I was framed in. If I could explain everything from 10 through 20 exactly what would I tell little Eudese, For even without words I know she wouldn't want to grow up to be Eudese In my own skin Sometimes sick to my stomach I want to step out of me So I know that little wouldn't want to be me I wish this didn't have to end so depressing but Honestly if the younger me were to appear in front of me today. Hopefully the song of my tears can be enough words said Dear Eudese words written by me to me Surround by childhood pictures and childhood memories Sincerely yours Eudese

Chapter 5 - Today is Me,Tomorrow is Growth

My God

When I mumble
When I whisper
When no one is around

When I seem dazed
Staring deeply into the eyes of the sky
When you're about to label me crazy
With a side of psychotic
Staring me down with your judgemental eyes
Understand I am talking to no other but My GOD

When I toss my hands in the air
Falling, collapsing , like a sick person to their knees
When my hands come together
Know that I am coming together with My GOD

When I put my fingers to the keyboard
When I put pen to paper
Without a thought about it
And the words flow like water and wine
Understand that it is no other than My GOD writing through me
Using me as his voice
No one other than My GOD

Battle The Balance

Bones rattling their cry for help
Promises of soothing comfort
With the warmth of the sun
Singing sweet sounds through the cracked window, soft whispers of
hushes
Comforting my aches and pains
Silencing all of my I don't wanna adult today's
Raising the tones of But you have to
Nights blankets have folded their selves

Into mornings smells of life awaiting you on the table for breakfast
A game of tug o war has begun yet again
Waking up turns into I can lay for ten more minutes
Ten more minutes turns into
On today's episode of not wanting to leave
I'm picking out my outfit from my bed
Snoozing for the commercial breaks
A toss and turn and we are live again
The rope gets tighter
Responsibility obligations promises
Makes my blood race in my palms
I'm already ready to nap for tomorrow
Sipping Pina coladas on my day off

Ladies Night

Don't ask me about my man tonight
From the moment my heels drop a beat on my porch step I'm single
I am rubbing oils on my cocoa butter skin
I am switching nursery rhymes to the wine and go down riddim
I am calling the girls and forget that
Let me tell you what he did
We talking about what we gonna do
The pre game before the real games
Have wine glass in one hand
While I wave the other and twerk my thang
No class
No behavior
I'm slinging the jeans in the hamper
Tonight, it's ladies night
The too much pride to hide these hands aren't big enough to hold
these thighs
Are coming out
It's ladies night
From fros to natural curls to crochet
We finna make America great again with our black woman magic
I am turning the lipstick up
As loud as my speakers
Red or plums, these shades will meet fame just from the kiss of my
lips
It's ladies night
I am me
We are us
Don't ask us about our man
They are their own
We are our own
Until we come home
Stumbling
Slurring dessert is on me tonight
Don't ask
And we won't tell
It's ladies night

Shoe's and Lipstick

Before you rise, Good Morning
As you lay in bed and ponder, Let me just say with the right
shoes and Lipstick you can conquer the world

While you swing your legs to the bedside, Blindly feel for
your glasses
Remember all will be in your view
The sun will shine it's light for you
The little birdies tweet tweet tweet will sing the day's mystery
The wind will roar out the courage within
Just remember with the right shoes and lipstick you got this

Power

If by a touch of a shoulder I could save a life
If by a wrap of my arms I can save a tear
If by the shine within my smile I can erase your worries
If by the truth in my eyes I can reassure you that everything will be alright
If the power of my love can outweigh
The heaviness of hate
Sisters would uplift each other
My brothers would stop shooting one another
Chalk would be used to draw out hopscotch instead of body outlines

If I could send clear tears of joy to Flint
If I can reveal reflections of toothless smiles and wrinkles that tell golden tales
If I can give water to float to your dreams

If I could tape up broken homes
Father and mother in every family portrait
Grandmothers and grandfathers in every rocking chair
With a loving lap and story to be shared
If I could build a home out of love…

If just my thoughts can cure hunger
My dreams fill bellies of babies
Napping on empty hopes

If I can show just one black girl
That she is unapologetically beautiful
And young black boy that he is a king in training

If by a kiss on the heart
I can send cures of promise
An obituary will be in the papers for diabetes
A funeral held for cancer
Rest peacefully out of our bodies leukemia

HIV would receive no transfer
Aids would have no skills to swim in our blood

If by the drip of my ink
Illusions of no one listening
Can reveal that my ears are listening
My heart is untying your young soul from
The tree limb where words unspoken lay, yet tears shed drip

Blood from the hands of an unloved child drop
Get down
And stand up for yourself child
If the power lived through me
I'd cradle this world in my hands of love

Today I slay

If today I awake
Today I am going to slay
If today the sun sing's
Today my butter pecan lipstick will be my mic
If today the cool breeze sway's my locs
My curls are going to vibe with my stride
If today cars are driven with window's down
Neighbor's are on their porch, Ice dancing in glasses
Electric sliding in lemonade
I am going to walk the runway of the sidewalk slaying
Melanin shining brighter than street lights when calling the youngins home
Today I am going to slay
Today what is my fat is my fluff
What is my short is my fun size
What is my scar is my story
What There is to me is going to be me
What there is to slay, I will slay it, murder it and put it to rest
Because for today, Once I've done it, there is no competition

About Author

You Never know who needs to hear your story , who needs to hear your poetry. I was raised in Boston Ma. My love for writing was born in Roxbury Ma on Holborn street in a little blue house where I grew up. Thanks to Ms. Ross. Another thanks to my Nana for constantly asking me what the sense of writing is when all I am going to do is keep them in a drawer? Reading other writer's stories and poetry took me places, kept my imagination going, my vision of the world differently. From ***Dr.Suess*** to ***Amelia Bedelia*** , to ***Hoops***, to ***Drama High*** , the ***Bluford series*** , ***Chicken Noodle Soup***, to ***Addicted*** to the ***Coldest Winter Ever***… down to even ***Webster dictionary*** . I can say I been places just by reading and as a writer I want to take my readers on a journey as well

About Books of Hope Boston

BOHB Is a branch of Books of Hope. Founded in 1999 by author and educator Anikah Nailah. Books of Hope has collectively published over 140 books of poetry, short- fiction, essays, plays, memoir, and hip- hop lit, written by all ages.

A literacy empowerment program that brings creative writing workshops to at-risk urban and immigrant youth and adults in the communities where they live, BOHB trains its participants in four key areas: writing, publishing, performance and entrepreneurship. They are mentored by professional writers, artists, and educators, and their writing is made public through readings at schools and events.

For more Information about Books of Hope Boston, to give a donation, purchase books, or volunteer, contact Tyler Barbosa, Program Director at tyoung@lenaparkcdc.org. Join us in empowering the next generation of authors, poets and artist at Lena Park community development center.

BOHB Acknowledgements

Books of Hope Boston is a collaborative program of Lena park Community development, has received generous support from Boston Cultural Council, a local agency which is supported by the Massachusetts Cultural Council, a state agency.

www.ingramcontent.com/pod-product-compliance
Lightning Source LLC
Chambersburg PA
CBHW031002090426
42737CB00008B/648